Book of Altars

Poems

Clara Bush Vadala

BELLE POINT PRESS

Fort Smith, Arkansas

Book of Altars

Cover image: *Anatomy of lymph vessels in dog* (1917–1918), Hermann Baum

Edited by Casie Dodd
Design & typography by Belle Point Press

Belle Point Press, LLC
Fort Smith, Arkansas
bellepointpress.com
editor@bellepointpress.com

Find Belle Point Press
on Facebook, Substack,
and Instagram (@bellepointpress)

Printed in the United States of America

28 27 26 25 24 1 2 3 4 5

ISBN: 978-1-960215-12-3

CHAP11/BPP24

At the altar of severed limbs

9000 dollars for a cat's thin leg
In the bag with the cold rabbit,
Caught by a different wild animal,
Its leg dangling with bacteria,
Greyhound tail in a towel, the 3rd
Bitten by another greyhound,
Finally caught in the act,
Hind limb, at the hip joint
Covered in cancer, shoulder
Broken in three places,
Toe, phalanges, another tail
Refusing to heal, the suture
Is the same each time, all
Of them but the rabbit
And the cat, still kicking
All their other limbs,
Sometimes other things
Removed—teeth, organs,
Pieces of intestine, how
Precious of each living thing
To give up their limbs and insides
Under anesthetics, how indecent

Of their bodies to give way
To all of it, without warning,
How extraordinary that each
One wakes without dysphoria
To keep on going and going.

At the altar of fragility

I.

The baby picks the flowers
With her whole fist, and yet
When her hand uncurls
The petals are not crushed

At all, but seem to unfurl
With her fingers. Even the stem
Is still there, and long enough
To put behind her ear and hold

The wild, white hair back.

II.

In the prairie, wild strawberries
Grow. Though they are the size
Of a thumbnail, they are sugary
Enough for bears to carefully pluck

Them from the vine, thin as the tail
Of a field mouse, without breaking
The fruit. Or, at least, this is what we assume,
Where there were strawberries yesterday,

The empty vine is not even stained red.

At the altar of the memory of the hammerhead

The pull of the shark
is sharp, convincing, the thick hook
slung deep behind his teeth.

My kid skin, made of silk,
strokes the barb-leather shark's
back, its salt-scale sandpapering

my hand. As the sun goes
down, the older boy on the beach
dumbly jumps to shove the thick clot

of his fist into its teeth, and I wish
I'd hissed *He's still alive,* my white
hair shaking in the wind, pale

as the inside of his gills. I touch
his belly as if my fingers could cut
him like a paring knife,

but we do not gut this fish.
Instead I shimmer into fish, wade
my waist into the surf—the shark

hovers over my hands a moment
I am more than mammal,
then hammers his flat head

into the sea. Another day,
I make my name in the sand
and let it be swept away.

The tide holds my name
in its mouth—even now,
I can still taste the salt.

At the altar of Histoplasma capsulatum

Inside the cells of the cat's wounded bone
there is something only a microscope can
name—the cat is named for what happened

to it. Roady. Found on the roadside road-
rashed, road-savvy enough to have not died,
instead living twice, as an animal and a fungal

incubator. The next time I see the cat, its leg
is healed, but it is still bleeding from its toes
where it scraped the carrier door in the car

all the way to the clinic. At the clinic, claws
fall out of the front seat; she has scratched them
out of her, finding herself on the road, again.

At the altar of accidental death and dismemberment

The pig's legs
We learned
To suture
On—because
The bruising
Breaks banana
Peels before
The knot
Can be tied—
Came pickled
In a jar, cloven
With garlic
And hooves
Softened
With vinegar,
The most
Similar to
Human skin
We might
Ever get

Even after
Graduation
Unless there
Is some mass
Casualty event
In which we
Must learn
Again to
Work in
Masks without
Coughing or
Sputtering
About the smell
We may or
May not
Still have
To endure.

At the altar of where the grass is really greener

And the Christmas tree is really green all year
And not spray-painted green and missing all its needles
And decorated with recycled cans of Lone Star beer
And chain-link fence toppers with decorated wood
Duct-taped to the side of them. At the altar where
The cattle don't need a shovel to break their water
Into palatable pieces, where the tortoise has 1/6
An acre to do its grazing, where nightshade only
Grows in pastures where no one is going to eat it
Accidentally. At the altar where the grass becomes
A tiny wheel with thorns, where little white flowers
Spot the yard, where ants excavate after rain,
Remaking their mounds, malleable and unearthly.
Where the last of the sugary hummingbird feeders
Expires into something that would keep even
The most devoted bird from being sober. At this
Altar, the yard comes to be clean shaven in summer,
To prepare for its job of greening, and greenering
The grass beside it, and beside that, and beside that.

At the altar of the witch's book at the Texas library sale

Are you sure you're old enough for that book
And then the snatch of some old and wrinkled
Hand toward me. Then I turn away and mutter
Some incantation or spell I've already learned
In the backyard with a discarded bottle of apple
Flavored Crown Royal and a tincture of wild
Onion and red pepper flakes mixed with water.
At this age, in this state, it's all of the secrets
I still have for myself. I put a cover on the book
After my parents buy it for me while the seller
Gives them the kind of glare that blesses every
Heart in a 10-mile radius with a pang of sorrow
They can't quite explain, but point it out to each
Child nearby, say God is telling us this is what we
Must do, raise your hands in His church and sing
Some kind of Christian pop. When I am 11, I ask
For a vanilla bean, whole, rock salt, a velvet bag
To keep close to my heart, to keep the ghosts out.

At the altar of the lingering heat

Bless the dog
Who vomits
Leather skins
Of its prey
    Teeth stained
    From coffee
    Breath ripe
With bitterness
Bless every feather
And peach pit
    Collected
    In Halloween
    Bucket long after
Halloween has
Passed and bless
The creature
    Chasing leaves
    Like they are birds
    And bless the birds
Cackling, warbling
At the creature's
Stupidity

From their roost
Bless each talon
On the wire table
On the porch
Which is not a porch
But planks of wood
Bless the hot
Toddy in his hand
While the other
Tends the flames
Licking the air
Bless the tongue
Of smoke not from
Something living
Burning and bless
Every dead thing
The bright air and the dark
Night and bless
The marbled moon
And its sisters the big
Bright stars and the firefly
Lighting behind itself
Bless everything left
In the wake of that light

At the altar of eventual blood

In the bathroom we say *Bloody Mary*
Three times to the mirror before
We've even had our period
Of time where we rely on things
Made of possible cotton and adhesive
Sticking to our underwear.

While we wait for Mary to tell us
Whether our wombs will be blessed
With carrying or doomed to empty
Themselves every month, *Bloody*
Mary, Bloody Mary, Bloody Mary
I guess it was six times we said it,

The school bus is waiting and we were told
It only takes seconds, at most, minutes
To pee. Before someone comes looking
For us, the air freshener at the top of the door
Hisses like an angry ghost and makes us
Scream and run out of the stalls without

Washing our hands. There is still
A small amount of the bathroom soap
On my hands. Why do I feel like I need
To hide it? I rub my hands together, then
On the leather of the bus seat back,
Then I say a little prayer, please, don't tell.

At the altar of the lingering cold

The arboretum's pansies are upset,
Their little lion faces frowning gold
And brown, their eyebrows furrowed, stamen set
Like jaws for pollen yet to come. The cold

Has crept along the soil too long and bees
Are late, but coming soon. In fact, one down
The trail has thighs all fattened orange and neon
Inside asparagus, a sugar crown

Anointing him a specific insect joy
Before the crown is passed to queen. Oh, how
This happiness could buzz the pansies coy
And satisfied! But spring is coming down

Hard, a viral pang opening the sky
To fever air, dead, sweet fruit bloat with flies

At the altar of the brooding hen

Chickens keep a specific grief like heat
Keeps chicks asleep, christening combs, deepening fat
Chicks under other mothers'
Wings

Cramped corral keeps chicks asleep
Under heat

Cold keeps creeping, choana slickens
In thick water
Keeps food medicated
For coccidiosis
Beak keeps spilling crumbles—sick
Tracks carve scaled feet, keep
Follicles from feathering this chicken's skin

This chicken's sick, broody in the coop
Roosts near the roof, keeps
Watch but falls asleep
A creature made for killing's
Crept in nest
Snakes
Eggs

Candles held against them cast
Embryonic caricatures, lacking
Chalaza, yolk sinks
Chicken keeps
What it can keep

Chicks are just a click from cracking shell
Muscles thick on necks made just for this

Chicken keeps a secret: egg
Inside, Chicken keeps a secret
Albumin leaks its sticky fluid
Chicken keeps concocting these excuses
Chicken keeps a secret, deep
A secret that will kill her

At the altar of imagined domestication

A news title reads "only a human
skull and a pair of pants" left after
the elephant kills the rhino

poacher and lions eat the remains.

When the rabbit dies the cat stretches
all its slender limbs in satisfaction

one wild thing to another.

The old coyote in the yard is in charge

of starting the midnight serenade.

Dominion does not include the wolf spider.

Unfortunately, it is more like the mother

of feral pigs dead on the roadside.

It is more like the loose dog watching

all her spotted piglets scrambling into brush,
less and less like the mother, the further they run.

It is more like when we hear about

the tamarins missing from the Dallas Zoo,
the snow leopard's escape, the lappet-faced
vulture dead of a suspicious wound.

At the altar of the emu farm

The emu only kicks if your hold fails
to keep it feeling safe. It's like a hug,
the way you wrap around it—from the tail
end first, then toward the beak, keep feet dug

in, flip it on its side. It can kick hard
every direction from the front or side,
but never from behind. This is because
the knees and hocks are made for flight;

no, not the winged way, the way in which prey
are evolutionarily designed
to do. There's a reason emus can wait
to change their strategy until the time

is ripe for using talons—no one here
believes the ratites have forgotten these.

At the altar of the sea otter

Nothing is sacred, not even what we used to call love
The small hand cupped within another palm
Not even the oyster eaten before it has time
To form a pearl, not even the pearl, like a slow-release
Antacid, swallowed into a stomach curdled as the sea
With the kind of acid that burns holes, cauterizes
The heart, not even the heart, pearl dissolving,
Pearl splinters breaking bit by bit and traveling
Along mucosa, into capillary beds, toward the heart
Not even this heart, starred and spangled with pieces
Of the perfect contents of an oyster, not even the pearl
Calms the curdled mass of blood and muscle, not even
The act of it, scarred by teeth the color of pearl, sharp
As their shards, drowned by the small hand, furred
And clawed and endlessly, endlessly devastating,
Not even the murder, not even the obsession,
Not even the sea or its wide, or its isolation,
Not even the kelp warping the drift, wrapping
The mammal to its altar, not even the mammal,
Never the mammal: unforgivable pearl of violence

At the altar of the dead and dying

After "Our Business Is Killing," Slate, *Feb. 2023:*
"If you must do one thing flawlessly in your career, it's killing."

If you knew what it was like to pronounce the dead
Gecko warmed crisp and bloodless after the ice storm
Thawed with a hair dryer because nothing is dead
Until its warm and dead heart under stethoscope beats
Slower slower stopping stops rabbit grabbed by neighbor's
Dog squealing turtle run over in the road and having to be
Sure there is no heartbeat by God or doppler before it goes
Into the freezer for cremation services to pick up dogs
With neurologic disorders waking even with dead hearts
To gasp and sometimes seize or sit up someone cataloguing
All the drugs and someone crying someone holding the foot
Of the creature someone standing at a distance someone
Covering the back end with a blanket so nothing is seen
That shouldn't be then the eyes of course which do not
Close sometimes you would not light a candle at every one
Of these altars instead you would light just one a red one
And watch the wax deteriorate until it burns itself out, burns
The dish it sits on covering everything in its gluey residue
You would not cry unless you had a moment in between

And then you would not cry unless the moment wasn't long
Enough to say goodbye and still you would not let yourself
Have this simple pleasure not even at the altar of all this
Over and over sorrow not even as the vein collapses and
Keeps you from giving the good death like you know how
The good death that comes swiftly the good death they deserve

At the altar of apology

Sometimes my tongue is thick
like that—
marine between my teeth,
thing like an eel,
slippery,
underneath it, only deeper things
that I can find no words for.

Planning to. Planning to say
Something—tongues get in the way.

A blue whale's
tongue
can weigh
two tons

the hypoglossal nerve
is a non-elastic sliver
in a normal mammal;
a whale's? The nervous twinge is electric

enough to power a human body
but speech remains impossible as
    sonar;

imagine speaking into quintillions
of gallons of water—the strength
of your tongue
having to travel
whole nautical miles—
as every fin and scale
marimbas with the sound

if my tongue
were two tons
it would still

be a human's tongue
in a whale's mouth

I still wouldn't have
the nerve
to say it.

At the altar of the broken-winged boat-tailed grackle

in the Walmart parking lot
the inhabitants of the ecosystem
startle.

The grackles are watching
their sister stand underneath
the car where she

has fallen with the French fries
from the pocket of the car door
that smacked her there.

Her wing is malpositioned,
feathers fluffed, each muscle
in each follicle standing

them on end. In the end
they are wrong to watch her
and do nothing

the way I do when I hear
what sounds like a jaguar
or a jungle possum

cackling and screeping,
and realize it is just a black bird
with a boat tail

and a broken wing calling
all the wild things
to the spectacle of her

knowing she will die, but
it will probably be slow
or at the hand

of a cat, or a fox like the one
I once saw near the bleachers,
flinging its prey

and yipping in glee, learning
how to play, to revel in the fear
of those weaker than it.

At the altar of the end of the world

First a person has to care
that I exist in the back
of this coffee shop—
then the sound of cutting
muscle on my laptop
will alert them I am
studying something
private, a surgery

on the hind limb
of a canine wracked
with cancer. Second, they
must assume I am
socialized. And not,
like so many strays,
feral. A product of a viral
illness which makes me,

in the way of the street dog,
averse to any kindness,
lest it be a predatory
diversion aimed to slip

innocence out of me
in the form of a choke chain.
Now last, the intention—
I will stare a curse into you

Old woman with the bible,
Man in the car outside.
Now I have mother's instinct
Inside me like a wolf, ready
to tear your scheme
to pieces—I have heard
of too many howls
curdled into screams

so look me in the eyes,
watch them turn gold—
ask me again, if you dare,
my relationship to Christ,
and realize it is too late,
it has always been this
way. Realize—we are already
here after the rapture.

At the altar of every little deity

the God of the day is of thunder and rain
the night after storms set dogs to itching
and whining let us out they demand and
we relent God of height God of Oak fertility
deity something about a lady drowning
in honey fat a dead bumblebee on the
back porch in the radish pot in folksong
the devil is just like a radish hammered
into the ground with a crack of thunder
and we are just hungry for something with
a little sting this is God is a tiny man and
the devil is like a long shadow as the sun
slips behind a thunderhead caterpillar folds
to nothing unimpressive brass gorilla rubbed
too smooth to grab any hair down comes the
greening rain patinas every copper thing

At the altar of the opposite of forgiveness

I hope you've forgiven
Me for knowing

Internal decapitation
Is an acceptable form

Of euthanasia
For poultry

That I have a pair
Of testicles

On a shelf
In formalin

And a collection
Of skulls of animals

So I can read
The difference

In their teeth
I hope you've forgiven

How many times
I say teeth

As if they are
The only bones

At the altar of the black dog

At which I say I don't want to hit him and the man says you're better than me, I would've just kept going. You should just keep going, go or you'll be here all day. And so I am here all day and I don't tell the man I am a veterinarian, because what would it prove? I roll up my window and watch him shoveling in his yard. Over his shoulder and into the dirt, the spear of the shovel smacks again and again. I can't figure out what he's digging for. As the dog gets closer, I open the door a bit and see that his fur has frozen into tiny black icicles and his tongue is lolling. I realize there is only the illusion of a tail, short, bobbed, the rest only black hair. The dog crouches as if to leap over the car into the yard on the other side, where a female dog is shuffling her puppies under the hay to stay warm. That man is still at it with the shovel. The dog is still stop-motioning toward me, away, toward, away, toward, I realize, with the swing of the shovel, up, down, up, down. Just because the dog is eating out of the roadside ditch does not mean it is not in pain. What does the man want me to do? The dog will not just pixelate into something flat I can pass over. What will happen to the dog, sitting by the tire now, if I kiss him on the nose? Will my lips freeze there in the cold like a tongue to a light pole? Will the dog turn into a prince? Suddenly, the sun is setting, the roads are freezing over. As the dark curtain billows down from somewhere above, the black dog disappears within it, the shovel chinks the hard earth. The man is suddenly nowhere to be seen.

At the altar of the anecdotal

When the neighbor's garage light makes dark
of the stars, I close my eyes to see the stars
there instead, and I never open them again.

In the closed eye, there is no darkness, only
the dark. There is a dog, or three, but no birds,
and the dogs are only there because they feel

they need to be helpful. I can feel their hot breath
and their needling hairs, but I cannot touch them
for fear of the warmth coming back to me. Why?

This bitter pill each morning at the same time
tastes the same it always did, but there is no
non-anecdotal evidence of these side effects.

The doctor doesn't listen when I tell them
through an app that this one turns the stars off;
too many combinations of chemicals, hormones

whacking their drumsticks against the inside
of my skull. I listen with my eyes closed. Here:
take my autonomy and use it to rate the app

five stars. Here: I don't need therapy, I need
a way to fuck without the side effects
of stroke, or shooting stars through the soft

prey part of me, migrating foreign bodies,
pulling the light string on intimacy; my eyes
close one more time, believe me, oh, believe—

I have failed to open once again, a music box
without its ballerina twirling. I don't want
another child, this is all the evidence I need.

At the altar of artificial intelligence

AI creates a woman
And she is beautiful
In a calculated way
Her too many fingers
Clicking their nails
Across a cellphone
Screen. Without clothes
On, she is feline,
Nipples numerous too,
And ready for a litter.
To be born of her
Is to fear your mouth
Will not open wide
Enough to scream
Because there are
Too many teeth
And not enough soft
Tissues on the internet
To approximate
A tongue. Baring
That unforgettable
Smile, caterpillar brows,

Spaghetti-thick hair,
We're getting weird
Now with the nose;
Two nostrils too
Many get chapped
At twice the rate
And bleed. What else
Of hers doesn't bleed?
We already know
She cannot swim,
But do we know,
If she is made of someone
Else's skin from
Pictures posted too
Long ago to remember,
What she looks like
In a swimsuit, or do we
Know if she would even drown?

At the altar of the extraterrestrial

Face the shape of a neonatal cat,
Sans the ears, and like a cat, your nails
Are made of hypodermic needles to inject
All manner of fever-inducing germ
Even the cat, when rescued, spends time
In a domicile composed of chrome
Or chrome-colored likenesses of what
You came to earth in. The cat, like you,
Examines each new specimen it stumbles
Upon for what benefit it might afford them—
Food, shelter, or exactly three strokes
Of a finger along its soft belly. Thank
The furred foot of a cat for its ability
To be almost completely a silent thing—
The kind of cloaking device we are all
Most afraid of—something hiding in plain sight.
I'd imagine the piloerector muscles along the back
Are the same in your species, too.
What raises your hackles? Beams of light?
There must be a reason a cat's dish
And your ship are both called a saucer.

At the altar of the black parade

No this is not a song, nor is it something with a melody.
There is no reason for each branch of this fractured plum tree

To bear any dark fruit, purpling its limbs like a bruise
But here it is blackened with all of this sweetness, swooning

Us into it. Here it is beckoning with its dark, dry bark, split
In the middle as if burned by a lightning strike, it is built

Just for this kind of surviving. The night comes over, the wasps
Lilting their tongues and sheathing their stingers, the waste

Of them turning up in plump bites of plum skin later. When
The plums are black and soft in the middle, we carry ten

Of them back in our shirts, now stained by the ones we could
Not help but break open with our teeth first. If the tree could

Speak it would tell us what about the blackberries, what about
The pecans, the firm pears, why are you taking these from out

Here where they are turning from fluid to flesh like magic?
How dare you take my work, how dare I hold on to this

Life if every year my leaves drop their waxy bodies to the dirt,
If all my children eat the sticky sap of me just to be only worth

The way they taste? The color of them clotting over time
Into something edible is black, black as the last drop of slime

From the worms inside the core—as the deer's or dog's blood
In the asphalt of the road, this tree knows the color of that blood.

At the altar of the year of the rabbit

Everything is multiplying. It is what we are good at.
The moon completes its phases faster than we've ever seen.
The great sheet of ice above the stratosphere fractures
And lets its pieces fall toward us—femur on the asphalt,
Shoulder blade still covered in fur, fingernails tickling
Our ears like the sound of sleet on already-frozen streets.
The rabbit laughs its belly laugh, legs extending from
Its hips all the way down to the deepest valley of the earth
From their sitting place in the full moon, and out they topple.
When their paws hit the dirt, they name themself Jack and hop
Toward a baseball bat, remembering to dodge it after the last
Time they were here, and spiritualists wanted them for their feet,
And some woman for her rituals, and someone hungry
For his stew, cold for his pelt. My daughter's jacket is the hide
Of one of these creatures. I was struck by its softness,
Its delicate seams, the fact that I had not experienced the loss
Of all the rabbits in the wombs of mothers who had them
Taken for a kind of show and tell. I would not have bought
It, Jack, having known you would arrive this way, without
All your natural protectants, how many years of the rabbit
Did it take to skin you? What are you doing back again?

At the altar of a particular pleasure

In the rafters of the barn
is a dead possum.
The contractor finds it
doing his inspection
before we move in.
It is plastered flat
on one side and dehydrated
next to a hand-built
Santa's sleigh the previous
inhabitants also left
up there in weird pieces.
We let them leave the barn
full of garage sale leftovers
as part of the contract.
The possum peels off easily
with the flick of an old shovel
also found on the property.
He fits nicely in a shadow box.
His hand is mummified
into a thumbs up, and I place
a faded daisy made of silk
I found with him there.

There are more flowers
than we know what
to do with. I send a box of quilt tops
to a friend's mom. A couple
of denim pearl snap button-ups
to my dad. My mom patiently
waits for us to unload the sleigh,
the outdoor light-up deer,
the tens of strands of icicle lights
and some dainty pottery.
My grandmother sifts
the knick knacks until she can't
hold any more of them.
I watch the dust mites settle
over what is left—baby dolls'
heads, crochet paraphernalia,
a wreath the size of the front
of the whole house. Wooden stamps,
a beautiful lamp. The whisper
of something I could make,
maybe, one day, into, or out of,
or display, or keep, or keep, or keep.

At the altar of goodbyes

Leave me quaking
like the arrows we left in the quiver,
your arm undone at the elbow.
How the warmth rose golden over us,
a delicate omission of what we would brood over later.
It was lovely, the bird cutting into the sky, the wide arc
of your bow at such an angle that it cut the same
atmospheric seam, as you laughed, not paying enough
attention, and let something fly
that you shouldn't have. To everyone's surprise
it is not the caterpillar that comes undone in this story,
but the cormorant instead.
Tell me again why you don't hunt with a gun.
That it kills things too fast, or your finger is always
too ready on the trigger.
Leave me to blacken my hands
with this bird, your arrow still moving in its chest.

At the altar of the cumulative weakening of trees

Domestic pets are getting fatter
In the hibernations forced upon them
During weather extremes, and trees
Are getting weaker freezing, thawing,
Freezing again. It is a drought year
Next, and the vegetation is allowed
To overgrow the telephone poles
And power lines. The next few months
We cut it all down mid-branch,
To keep leaves from shading solar
Panels on the roof. This would violate
Me. In fact, it does. The rising and
Dropping of temperatures inside
The body of a person can shake
The equilibrium right out of you
Like elk shaking antlers off too early,
Before it is the time of year for shed.
Like peach pits hanging by a stem
In February, even though the peach
Tree never bore its fruit. Someone

Help us all to remember what green
Is and that the knockout roses don't
Smell like roses, even after generations
Of blooms, you'd think they would have
Evolved by now, forgot, instead have
Only grown more, and sharper, thorns.

At the altar of inevitable

Evidence of eventual extinction is everywhere
And everyone on earth is the exception, except
There are not exceptions for the inevitable,
Except, every evening each extinguishing star
Explodes in ecstasy at the experience of ethereal
Ending, except the extraordinary experience
Is anything but extraordinary, except it is like
An explosion, every ordinary existence exiting
At once and each exit has heavy exit signs red
And screeching. Evening, everyone, it is inevitable
That we are easily the most extinguishable species
And even the earth will not erase itself without us
Irreversibly entering it over and over and over

At the altar of bodies left behind

Thorax, abdomen, muscle
Covering the place where scapulae
Once lay flat like spatulas against
The horizontal rib cage. Bodies
Smacking bodies in the way
That dogs play, hide to hide.
These are all living bodies,
The altar moves within them.
There is a woman here, too
Feral, made out of approximations;
Her chest is littered with kittens,
Hungry and thin, queens missing
From their dominion of street-side
And alley-way. Inside the chest
Of the woman is a heavy thing
Closed up with lock and key;
The chest contains the ash
Of the body that left at a ripe age
After seizuring. The slap of skin
To skin wakes us, the baby
Crying for her milk, bodies
Made for feeding, bodies

Made for fleeing, bodies
Sutured and stapled back
Together at their warm seams
To pass along what kept them
Alive for all this time, despite.

Acknowledgments

Thank you to *Many Nice Donkeys* for publication of "At the altar of the broken-winged boat-tailed grackle." To my friends and family who encourage me, to my husband and daughter who inspire me, to all the animals I love and have yet to meet, and to science and medicine, my life's pursuit.

Clara Bush Vadala is a poet and veterinarian from Van Alstyne, Texas. She has work in various publications including *Iron Horse Literary Review*, *New South Review*, and *Moss Puppy* among others. She serves as associate poetry editor of *Thimble Literary Magazine* and works full time as a veterinarian. Clara lives with ten pets, 19 chickens, and her husband and daughter who graciously accept her love of animals to the fullest extent. Clara's full-length collection of poems *Resembling a Wild Animal* is forthcoming from ELJ Editions later this year (2024).